The Big Book Of Old Testament Bible Trivia

Cheryl Pryor

Arlington & Amelia Publishing

Arlington & Amelia Publishing

ISBN-10: 1-886541-33-7
ISBN-13: 978-1-886541-33-7

TABLE OF CONTENTS

OTHER BOOKS BY CHERYL PRYOR

The Big Book of New Testament Bible Trivia

The Big Book of Presidential Trivia

The Big Book of First Ladies Trivia

Presidents, First Ladies, & First Family Trivia

Presidents Trivia Challenge

First Family Trivia

American Revolution & The Birth of A Nation Trivia

Living The Word of God

Chosen

Children Of The Presidents

Pregnancy Journal

Precious Moments

Treasured Moments of My Child

My Mother's Life Story

My Father's Life Story

How Much Do You *Really* Know About The Love Of Your Life?

Couples Game Night Challenge

RV Travel & Expense Journal

Wedding Survival Guide

Write Now

Legacy

Children's Books

My Child's Keepsake Journal

Trivia For Kids: The Presidents

Trivia For Kids: First Ladies

From the series: The Sullivan Family Series

Savannah In The Big Move

Savannah On Stage

Savannah On Horseback

Savannah in Look What Followed Me Home

Savannah & The Grumpy Neighbor

Savannah & The Mad Scientist

From the series: Savannah's World Travels Series

Savannah's Disney World Celebration

Savannah Goes To Paris

Pentateuch

1

GENESIS

Answers on page 8 - 10

1. On what day did God create vegetation, such as plants and trees?

2. What did God form man from?

3. A river flowed out of the garden of Eden and divided into four rivers. Can you name the four rivers?

4. From what tree did God command man not to eat from?

5. God made woman from what part of man?

6. Who, or what, enticed Eve to eat of the fruit of the tree that God had forbidden them to eat from?

7.Who was the first born child of Adam and Eve?

8. Adam and Eve's sons, Cain and Abel, one was a keeper of flocks and the other was a tiller of the ground. Which was a keeper of flocks?

9. How many years did Adam live?

10. Which son of Adam and Eve responded to God when asked where his brother was, “Am I my brother's keeper?” after killing his own brother?

11. Name the three sons of Noah who were with him on the ark.

12. God was sorry He had made man on the earth and said, “I will blot out man whom I have created from the face of the land, from man to animals to creeping things and to birds of the sky, for I am sorry I have made them.” Who found favor in the eyes of God, who He did not blot out from the face of the land?

13. What type of wood was used to make Noah's ark?

14. What did God tell Noah to take into the ark with him?

15. How many days of rain were there while Noah was on the ark?

16. On what mountain did Noah's ark come to rest?

17. What sign did God tell Noah would be a sign of the covenant that never again would the waters flood and destroy all mankind?

18. What were men building when God confused the language of the earth and scattered the people over the face of the earth?

19. In the war of the kings, when the kings of Sodom and Gomorrah fled, what happened to them?

20. What was the name of Sarai's (Sarah) maid that she gave to Abram (Abraham) to conceive a child?

21. What was the name of Abram's son with the maid Hagar?

22. When Sarah heard that at age 90 she would have a child, what was her reaction?

23. Who warned Lot to take his family and leave Sodom?

24. Lot and his family while fleeing Sodom were warned not to look back, but his wife disobeyed. What happened to her?

25. What was the name of the son of Abraham and Sarah?

26. What did God tell Abraham to offer as a burn offering in the land of Moriah to test Abraham?

27. What was the name of Isaac's wife?

28. What were the names of the twins of Isaac and his wife?

29. In exchange for what, did Esau sell his birthright to his brother Jacob?

30. How did Jacob deceive his father Isaac, in order to steal his brother Esau's blessing?

31. How was Jacob deceived by Laban, his mother's brother?

32. Which of Jacob's wives stole the household idols belonging to her father?

33. What did God change Jacob's name to?

34. What was the name of Jacob and Leah's daughter who was taken by force by Shechem, son of Hamon the Hivite?

35. How did Jacob's sons, Simon and Levi, repay Hamon and his son Shechem for defiling their sister?

36. For which son did Israel make a multi-colored tunic?

37. Which brother of Joseph saved him from his brother's plot to kill him?

38. Joseph's brothers sold him to Midianite traders in exchange for what?

39. Two officials of the Pharaoh had their dreams interpreted by Joseph. Who were they or what were their official duties?

40. When the Pharaoh had Joseph interpret his dream, what did he tell him the seven fat cows followed by seven gaunt cows represented?

41. During the famine when Jacob sent his sons to Egypt to buy grain, which son was kept behind?

42. Who were Israel's sons with his wife Rachel?

43. What were Joseph's brothers response when Joseph revealed to them that he was their brother?

44. Why did Joseph tell his brothers not to be angry with themselves for selling him as a slave?

45. Name the twelve tribes of Israel.

Answers – Chapter 1 – Genesis

1. The third day of creation – Genesis 1: 13

2. Dust - Genesis 2: 7

3. Pishon, Gihon, Tigris, and the Euphrates – Genesis 2: 10 – 14

4. The tree of knowledge of good and evil – Genesis 2: 16 – 17

5. Rib – Genesis 2: 2

6. Serpent – Genesis 3: 1 – 5

7. Cain – Genesis 4: 1

8. Abel was the keeper of flocks – Genesis 4: 2

9. 930 years – Genesis 5: 5

10. Cain – Genesis 4: 9

11. Shem, Ham & Japheth – Genesis 5: 32

12. Noah – Genesis 6: 6 – 8

13. Gopher wood – Genesis 6: 14

14. Noah and his sons, Noah's wife, his son's wives, and of every living thing two of every kind and food – Genesis 6: 18 – 21

15. 40 days and 40 nights – Genesis 7: 4

16. Ararat – Genesis 8: 4

17. A bow in the cloud (rainbow) – Genesis 9: 8 – 17

18. Babel – a city and a tower that would reach heaven – Genesis 11: 4 – 9

19. They fell into tar pits – Genesis 14: 10

20. Hagar – Genesis 16: 1 – 3

21. Ishmael – Genesis 16: 15

22. She laughed – Genesis 18: 10 – 12

23. Two angels – Genesis 19: 1, 13

24. She turned into a pillar of salt – Genesis 19: 26

25. Isaac – Genesis 21: 3

26. His son Isaac – Genesis 22: 1 – 2

27. Rebekah – Genesis 24: 67

28. Esau and Jacob – Genesis 25: 24 – 26

29. Stew – Genesis 25: 29 – 33

30. His mother Rebekah prepared a stew to serve him and he wore his brother's clothing and his mother put the skins of kid goats on his hand and neck to make him appear hairy as his brother Esau. - Genesis 27: 1 – 29

31. He had worked for him for seven years in order to marry his younger daughter Rachel, but Laban replaced her with his older daughter Leah. - Genesis 29: 18 – 28

32. Rachel – Genesis 31: 19

33. Israel – Genesis 32: 27 – 28, 35: 10

34. Dinah – Genesis 34: 1 – 2

35. They killed them while they were in pain from being circumcised along with every other male in the city and then they looted the city. - Genesis 34: 14 – 29

36. Joseph – Genesis 37: 3

37. Reuben – Genesis 37: 20 – 22

38. Twenty shekels of silver – Genesis 37: 28

39. The baker and the cup bearer – Genesis 40: 8 – 19

40. Seven years of abundance followed by seven years of famine –

Genesis 41: 15 – 30

41. Benjamin – Genesis – 42: 1 – 4

42. Joseph and Benjamin – Genesis – 42: 4, 43: 29

43. Dismayed – Genseis 45: 1- 4

44. God sent him to the home of Pharaoh to preserve their lives during the famine. - Genesis 45: 5 – 8

45. Reuben, Simeon, Levi, Judah, Zebulon, Issachar, Dan, Gad, Asher, Naphtali, Joseph, and Benjamin – Genesis 49: 1 – 28

2

Exodus

Answers on page 15 - 17

1. When a new king came into power who did not know Joseph, how did he deal with the sons of Israel?

2. What did the king of Egypt tell the Hebrew midwives to do at the birthing of a Hebrew woman?

3. What did the mother of Moses do to save her infant son?

4. Who found and raised Moses as her own?

5. Why did Pharaoh try to kill Moses?

6. What was the name of Moses' wife, a daughter of the priest of Midian?

7. How did the Lord appear to Moses?

8. What was the Lord's message to Moses that He delivered from the burning bush?

9. When Moses asked God what to tell the sons of Israel when they asked, 'What was His name,' what was His response to Moses?

10. What was the name of Moses' mother?

11. When Moses went before Pharaoh and Aaron took his staff and threw it down, what did the staff turn into?

12. When Pharaoh hardened his heart and wouldn't listen, Moses turned the water in the Nile into what?

13. How many of the ten plagues can you name?

14. What did God command the Israelites to do with the blood of the Passover lamb?

15. What was the blood of the Passover lamb on the lintel and doorposts a sign for?

16. When Pharaoh let the Israelites go, what was the reason God did not lead them by the land of the Philistines?

17. Whose bones did Moses carry with him?

18. In what form did God lead the Israelites out of Egypt?

19. After the Israelites left Pharaoh and the Egyptians chased them, how did the Israelites escape?

20. What happened to Pharaoh's men who were chasing the Israelites?

21. What sea was parted by Moses for the Israelites to flee from Pharaoh and the Egyptians?

22. Moses and Aaron's sister was a prophetess. What was her name?

23. What did God provide the Israelites to eat while they wandered in the wilderness?

24. When Amalek came and fought against Israel at Rephidim, Israel prevailed as long as Moses did what?

25. What was the name of Moses' father-in-law who was also the priest of Midian?

26. What was the name of the mountain where God met with Moses giving him the Ten Commandments?

27. How many of the Ten Commandments can you name?

28. *Fill in the blanks.* What were the boundaries the Lord gave to the

Israelites: from the ____________ Sea to the sea of the ___________, and from the wilderness to the River ___________.

29. How long was Moses on Mount Sinai in the midst of the cloud of the glory of God?

30. From what type of wood was the Ark of the Covenant made?

31. While Moses was on Mount Sinai, the people came to Aaron and asked him to make them a god. What did they make?

32. When Moses saw the idol the people had made and saw them dancing, what did Moses do?

33. When Moses came down from Mount Sinai, due to Moses speaking with God what did the others notice about him when he came down from the mountain?

34. The Ark of the Covenant was made of acacia wood and overlaid with what?

Answers – Chapter 2 – Exodus

1. The new king appointed taskmasters over them and afflicted them with hard labor. - Exodus 1: 8 – 11

2. If they gave birth to a son to put it to death, but if it was a daughter to let it live. - Exodus 1: 15 – 16

3. She hid him for three months and when she could hide him no longer she put him in a wicker basket and set it by the bank of the Nile. - Exodus 2: 2 – 3

4. The daughter of Pharaoh. - Exodus 2: 5 – 10

5. For killing an Egyptian who was beating a Hebrew – Exodus 2: 11 – 15

6. Zipporah – Exodus 2: 16 – 21

7. In a burning bush – Exodus 3:2

8. He heard the pleas of His people, the sons of Israel, and He came to deliver them from the Egyptians and deliver them to a land of milk and honey. - Exodus 3: 7 – 8

9. I Am Who I Am – Exodus 3: 13 – 14

10. Jochebed – Exodus 6: 20

11. Serpent – Exodus 7: 8 – 10

12. Blood – Exodus 7: 14 – 20

13. 1) Water turned to blood – Exodus 7: 20

    2) The land was filled with frogs -Exodus 8: 2

    3) Gnats throughout the land - Exodus 8: 16

    4) Swarms of insects – Exodus 8: 21

    5) Pestilence on the livestock – Exodus 9: 3

6) Boils on man and beast – Exodus 9: 8 – 9

7) Hail – Exodus 9: 18

8) Locusts – Exodus 10: 4 – 6

9) Darkness – Exodus 10: 21

10) Death of the firstborn – Exodus 11:5

14. Put the blood on the two doorposts and the lintel of their homes – Exodus 12:7

15. That no plague would touch them when the Lord struck the land of Egypt – Exodus 12: 13

16. When the people saw war they wouldn't change their minds and return to Egypt – Exodus 13: 17

17. Joseph – Exodus 13: 19

18. A pillar of cloud by day, a pillar of fire by night – Exodus 13: 21

19. Moses stretched out his hand over the sea and God turned the sea into dry land, so the waters were divided. The sons of Israel walked through the midst of the sea on the dry land. The waters were like a wall to them on both sides. - Exodus 14: 21 – 22

20. The waters came back down over them and not one of them survived. - Exodus 14: 23 – 28

21. Red Sea - Exodus 15: 4

22. Miriam - Exodus 15: 20

23. Manna – bread in the morning and meat at twilight (quail) - Exodus 16: 12, 31

24. Standing at the top of the hill he held his hand up with the staff of God in his hand. - Exodus 17: 8 – 11

25. Jethro - Exodus 18: 1

26. Mount Sinai - Exodus 19: 18

27. 1) You shall have no other gods before Me

2) You shall not make for yourself an idol

3) You shall not take the name of the Lord your God in vain

4) Remember the Sabbath day to keep it holy

5) Honor your father and your mother

6) You shall not murder

7) You shall not commit adultery

8) You shall not steal

9) You shall not bear false witness against your neighbor

10) You shall not covet

- Exodus 20: 3 – 17

28. From the Red Sea, to the sea of the Philistines, and from the wilderness to the River Euphrates - Exodus 23 31

29. 40 days and 40 nights - Exodus 24: 18

30. Acacia wood - Exodus 25: 10

31. A molten calf - Exodus 32: 1- 4

32. He threw the stone tablets and shattered them, he burned the calf and ground it to powder, scattered it over the water and made the Israelites drink it. - Exodus 32: 19 – 20

33. His face shone - Exodus 34: 29 – 30

34. Pure gold - Exodus 37: 1 - 2

3

Leviticus

Answers on page 20

1. What did Moses tell Aaron and his sons God commanded him to do so the glory of God would appear to the people?

2. Nadab and Abihu, the sons of Aaron, placed incense in their firepan and offered it before God, which He had not commanded them to do. What happened to them because of this?

3. When God spoke to Moses and Aaron in reference to the laws about animals for food, which of these did he say were creatures they could eat:

A. split hoof & chews the cud	*C. pig*
B. from the water that do not have fins & scales	*D. rabbit*

4. When a woman gives birth to a male child, for how many days is she considered unclean?

5. How many days after the birth of a male child should the flesh of the foreskin be circumcised?

6. The Lord God commanded, “You shall not lie with a male as one lies with a female.” What does the Lord God say of this act?

Answers – Chapter 3 – Leviticus

1. A burnt offering – Leviticus 9: 1 – 6; 9: 23

2. Fire came from the presence of the Lord God and consumed them. - Leviticus 10: 1 – 2

3. A – split hoof and chews the cud - Leviticus 11: 1 – 12

4. 7 days - Leviticus 12: 2

5. 8 days - Leviticus 12: 3

6. It is an abomination - Leviticus 18: 22; 20: 13

4

Numbers

Answers on page 24 - 25

1. Of the tribes of Israel, which was the only tribe not numbered in the census?

2. When a man or woman took a vow of a Nazarite, name one of the things he or she must agree to do.

3. The tent of the testimony where the tabernacle lay was covered by the cloud at night that gave the appearance of what?

4. What was the sign God gave the sons of Israel that it was time to move the camp?

5. Why did the people complain about manna?

6. What burden did Moses complain to the Lord God that had been laid upon him?

7. How did the Lord God relieve Moses of the burden of the sons of Israel

he led in the wilderness?

8. The Lord God told Moses to send out men to spy on what land?

9. When the spies returned, they reported seeing men of great size and stated they (the spies) were like grasshoppers in their sight. Who were these men of great size the spies described?

10. The Lord God pardoned the sons of Israel, those who had seen His glory and signs performed in Egypt; yet having put the Lord God to the test what punishment did the Lord God give them?

11. God did not permit those who had seen His glory and put Him to the test during their journey to come into the promised land. In return for their unfaithfulness they would wander how many years, never setting foot in the promised land?

12. Which servant of the Lord found favor in the Lord's sight and was allowed to enter the promised land?

13. The Lord told Moses for each of the sons of Israel to get a rod for each father's household and write their name on the rod. What was to be the sign on the rod of the man God chose?

14. What household's rod was chosen?

15. Where did Miriam, sister of Moses die?

16. At Meribah God told Moses to take the rod and for Moses and Aaron to assemble the congregation and speak to the rock and it would yield water. What did Moses do different from what God commanded?

17. Due to Moses not following the instruction of God to bring forth the waters at Meribah, what was the price Moses and Aaron paid?

18. Who was it whose donkey spoke to him after seeing the angel of the Lord?

19. What mountain did the Lord tell Moses to go up to see the promised land He gave to the sons of Israel?

20. Who did the Lord appoint to succeed Moses and to lead the people?

Answers – Chapter 4 – Numbers

1. The tribe of Levi – Numbers 1: 47 – 49

2. Any of the three below would be correct. - Numbers 6: 1 - 6

   1) Abstain from drinking wine and strong drink

   2) No razor shall pass over his head.

   3) He shall not go near a dead person.

3. Fire – Numbers 9: 15

4. When the cloud was lifted – Numbers 9: 17

5. They wanted meat, fruits, and vegetables. - Numbers 11: 4 – 6

6. The burden of the people. - Numbers 11: 11

7. 70 men of the elders of Israel. - Numbers 11: 16 – 17

8. Canaan – Numbers 13: 2

9. Nephilim – Numbers 13: 31 – 33

10. They would not see the land which He swore to their fathers. - Numbers 14: 20 – 23

11. 40 years – Numbers 14: 34

12. Caleb, son of Jephumneh and Joshua, the son of Nun – Numbers 14: 24, 30

13. The rod would sprout. - Numbers 17: 1 – 5

14. The rod of Aaron, for the household of Levi – Numbers 17: 8

15. Kadesh – Numbers 20: 1

16. He struck the rock twice. - Numbers 20: 8 – 11

17. They would not bring the assembly into the land the Lord gave them.

- Numbers 20: 12

18. Balaam – Numbers 22: 22 – 31

19. Abarim – Numbers 27: 12 – 13

20. Joshua, the son of Nun – Numbers 27: 15 – 18

5

Deuteronomy

Answers on page 28

Fill in the blanks for the first 5 questions.

1. You shall have no other ___________ before Me.

2. Honor your ___________ and your ___________.

3. You shall not commit ___________.

4. You shall love the Lord your God with all your ___________, and with all your ___________, and with all your ___________.

5. Man does not live by bread alone, but man lives by everything that proceeds out of the ___________ of the Lord.

6. What were the Ten Commandments written on?

7. Where were the tablets with the Ten Commandments kept?

8. What tribe carried the Ark of the Covenant?

9. What did the Lord tell the Israelites about the pig, as far as whether it was alright to eat it or not?

10. What was the remission of debt that was granted every seven years?

11. What did the Lord say about those who practice witchcraft?

12. What mountain did the Lord tell Moses to go up to see the land of Canaan, where Moses also died?

13. How old was Moses when he died?

Answers – Chapter 5 – Deuteronomy

1. Gods – Deuteronomy 5: 7

2. Father, mother – Deuteronomy 5: 16

3. Adultery – Deuteronomy 5: 18

4. Heart, soul, might – Deuteronomy 6: 5

5. Mouth – Deuteronomy 8: 3

6. 2 tablets of stone – Deuteronomy 10: 1

7. Ark of the Covenant – Deuteronomy 10: 2

8. The tribe of Levi – Deuteronomy 10: 8

9. It was unclean because it divides the hoof but does not chew the cud. -Deuteronomy 14: 8

10. Every creditor shall forgive the debt owed to him. - Deuteronomy 15: 1 – 2

11. Whoever does this is detestable to the Lord. - Deuteronomy 18: 10 – 12

12. The mountain of Abarim, Mount Nebo (in the land of Moab opposite Jericho). - Deuteronomy 32: 48 – 50

13. 120 years – Deuteronomy 34: 7

Historical

6

Joshua

Answers on page 32

1. Who was the harlot that housed the spies Joshua sent out to view the land?

2. What did the spies tell Rahab to do to protect her and her family?

3. What occurred when the waters of Jordan cut off the waters which were flowing down from above stood and rose in one heap and the people of Israel crossed on dry ground?

4. What did the twelve stones taken up from the middle of the Jordan signify?

5. How long did the sons of Israel walk in the wilderness?

6. At what point did the manna cease?

7. When Joshua was by Jericho he came upon a man standing with his sword drawn. Who was he?

8. The men of Israel marched around the city of Jericho for six days. On the seventh day, what happened when the priests blew their trumpets and the people shouted?

9. How did the inhabitants of Gibeon deceive the Israelites?

10. What was the purpose of the Gibeonites in deceiving the Israelites?

11. When Adonizedok, King of Jerusalem, learned Joshua captured Ai, he and four other kings attacked Gibeon. As they and their armies were being slaughtered and they fled from Israel, how did the Lord kill them?

12. On the day the Lord delivered up the Amorites before the sons of Israel, what happened to the sun?

13. What did Caleb say he would give to the man who attacked Kiriath-sepher and captured it?

14. A person who killed someone unintentionally could flee to this place, a place where he could dwell. What was it?

Answers – Chapter 6 – Joshua

1. Rahab – Joshua 2: 1

2. Tie a cord of scarlet thread in the window in which she let the spies down – Joshua 2: 12 – 19

3. When the soles of the feet of the priests who carried the Ark of the Covenant rested in the waters – Joshua 3: 12 – 17

4. They were to become a memorial to the sons of Israel because the waters of the Jordan were cut off before the Ark of the Covenant when it crossed the Jordan. - Joshua 4: 3 – 8

5. 40 years – Joshua 5: 6

6. The day after they had eaten the produce of the land. - Joshua 5: 12

7. Captain of the host of the Lord – Joshua 5: 13 – 14

8. The walls of the city fell. - Joshua 6: 1 – 20

9. They told Joshua they came from a very far country. - Joshua 9: 1 – 11

10. So their lives would be spared. - Joshua 9: 15 – 19

11. The Lord threw large hail stones from heaven on them. - Joshua 10: 1 – 11

12. The sun stopped in the middle of the sky and did not go down for a day. - Joshua 10: 12 – 14

13. His daughter (Achsah) as a wife – Joshua 15: 16

14. City of refuge – Joshua 20: 2 – 9

7

Judges

Answers on page36 - 37

1. After the death of Joshua, how did the sons of Israel do evil in the sight of the Lord?

2. How was Eglon the King of Moab killed?

3. How did Shamgar save Israel?

4. *Fill in the blank.* Deborah, wife of Lappidoth, judged Israel and was also a ______________.

5. How did Jael kill Sisera?

6. What did Gideon ask of the Lord to show that he would deliver Israel through Gideon?

7. How were the 300 men chosen who along with Gideon would deliver the Midianites?

8. When Abimelech went to his father Gideon's home to kill his 70 brothers, who of all the brothers survived?

9. What reason did Jephthah's brothers give for why he would not receive an inheritance from his father's house?

10. What vow did Jephthah give to the Lord in exchange for giving the sons of Ammon into his hand?

11. Who was the one to greet Jephthah upon his return, who he vowed to sacrifice for the Lord?

12. How did the men of Gilead test the fugitives wanting to cross the Jordan to see if they were from Ephraim?

13. When the angel of the Lord came to the barren woman and told her she would give birth to a son and no razor should come upon his head for he would be a Nazarite, who did the angel say the son would deliver Israel from?

14. What was the answer to Samson's riddle: "*Out of the eater came something to eat, and out of the strong came something sweet*"?

15. When Samson learned his wife had been given to another man, how did he retaliate towards the Philistines?

16. When Samson was bound and delivered to the Philistines for retribution, what happened to the Philistines?

17. Who did the Philistines ask to entice Samson to learn where his strength lie and how he could be overpowered?

18. What must be done in order for Samson to lose his strength?

19. How was Samson avenged?

20. What tribe was cut off from Israel?

Answers – Chapter 7 – Judges

1. They served other gods – Baal and the Ashtaroth. - Judges 2: 11 – 13

2. Sword - Judges 3: 17 – 22

3. He struck down 600 Philistines with an ox goad. - Judges 3: 31

4. Prophetess - Judges 4: 4

5. She took a tent peg and hammer and drove the peg into his temple. - Judges 4: 17 – 21

6. The fleece of the wool on the threshing floor would only have dew on it and be dry on the ground. The second thing he asked was for the fleece to be dry, but the threshing floor all around it to be wet with dew. - Judges 6: 36 – 40

7. Those were chosen who lapped the water by putting their hand to their mouth. - Judges 7: 2 – 7

8. Jotham, the youngest, for he hid. - Judges 9: 5

9. He was the son of a harlot, the son of another woman. - Judges 11: 1 – 2

10. Whoever came out of his house to meet him upon his return he would offer to the Lord as a burnt offering. - Judges 11: 29 – 31

11. His only daughter - Judges 11: 30 – 35

12. They would ask them to say "Shibboleth," and if they could not pronounce it correctly they would know they were an Ephraimite. - Judges 12: 5 - 6

13. The Philistines - Judges 13: 1 – 5

14. What is sweeter than honey? And, What is stronger than a lion? - Judges 14: 12 – 18

15. He caught 300 foxes and took torches, turned the foxes tail to tail, and put one torch in the middle between two tails, lit the torches, and

released the foxes into the grain of the Philistines, burning the shocks, standing grain, vineyards, and groves. - Judges 15: 1 - 5

16. With the jawbone of a donkey he killed 1,000 of them - Judges 15: 10 – 15

17. Delilah - Judges 16: 4 – 6

18. If his head was shaved he would lose his strength and be weak like any other man. - Judges 16: 17

19. He knocked the pillars down on which the house rested killing all the people inside, about 3,000 in all. - Judges 16: 25 – 30

20. Benjamin - Judges 21: 6

8

Ruth

Answers on page 40

1. Which of the two of Naomi's daughters-in-law stayed with her even after the death of Naomi's husband and sons? (When Naomi told her to return to her people, she said, 'Where you go, I will go, and where you lodge, I will lodge. Your people shall be my people, and your God my God.)

2. After the death of her husband and sons what did Naomi change her name to?

3. In whose field did Ruth glean among the ears of grain?

4. When Boaz treated Ruth with kindness, when Ruth asked him why did she find favor in his sight, how did he respond to Ruth's question?

5. What did Naomi tell Ruth to do the night Boaz was to winnow barley at the threshing floor in order to seek security for Ruth?

6. What was the custom at the time in Israel concerning the redemption and exchange of land and to confirm a matter?

7. Who did Ruth marry after the death of her first husband?

8. What was the name of their son?

Answers – Chapter 8 – Ruth

1. Ruth – Ruth 1: 3 – 16

2. Mara – Ruth 1: 20

3. Boaz – Ruth 2: 1 – 2

4. Because of all she did for her mother-in-law and left the land of her birth and came to people she did not know. - Ruth 2: 5 – 11

5. Put on her best clothes and when he laid down to uncover his feet and to lie down. - Ruth 3: 1 – 4

6. A man removed his sandal and gave it to another. - Ruth 4: 2 – 7

7. Boaz – Ruth 4: 9 – 13

8. Obed – Ruth 4: 17

9

First Samuel

Answers on page 44 - 45

1. What vow did Hannah make to the Lord if He would give her a son?

2. What did Eli the priest think when he saw Hannah praying and her lips were moving but no words came out of her mouth?

3. What did Hannah name her son?

4. Who fought and defeated Israel and took the Ark of the Covenant?

5. A man from battle gave Eli the news that Israel fled before the Philistines, his two sons were dead, and the Ark of God was taken. When the fate of the Ark of God was mentioned, what happened to Eli?

6. What did Eli's daughter-in-law, wife of his son Phinehas, say about Israel when she learned of the Ark of God being taken?

7. Why did the Philistines return the Ark of the Covenant to Israel?

8. Why did the Lord strike down some of the men of Beth-shemesh?

9. As Samuel grew old, what did the elders of Israel request of him to judge them?

10. Who did the Lord tell Samuel was the one who "shall rule over My people"?

11. Of what tribe was Saul?

12. When the Lord rejected Saul, who did He select and instruct Samuel to anoint?

13. When the Spirit of the Lord departed from Saul, what terrorized Saul?

14. What did David do when the evil spirit came to Saul to make it depart from him?

15. What weapons did David choose to use to fight against Goliath?

16. What was the name of Saul's daughter who became David's wife?

17. While Saul pursued David to kill him, where was he when David instead of taking Saul's life cut off the edge of Saul's robe?

18. What was the name of the wife of Nabal who David married after

Nabal's death?

19. Who did Saul ask the medium to bring up for him?

20. How did Saul die?

Answers – Chapter 9 – First Samuel

1. She vowed she would give him to the Lord all the days of his life and a razor shall never come on his head. - I Samuel 1: 11

2. He thought she was drunk. - I Samuel 1: 12 – 13

3. Samuel - I Samuel 1: 20

4. Philistines - I Samuel 4: 10 – 11

5. He fell off his seat backward, his neck was broken and he died. - I Samuel 4: 15 – 18

6. "The glory has departed from Israel." - I Samuel 4: 19 – 22

7. The Lord's hand was severe on them and on Dagon, their god. The Lord ravaged them with tumors. - I Samuel 5: 2 – 11

8. They looked into the Ark of the Covenant. - I Samuel 6: 19

9. A king - I Samuel 8: 4 – 5

10. Saul - I Samuel 9: 16 – 17

11. Benjamin - I Samuel 9: 21

12. The youngest son of Jesse, David. - I Samuel 16: 1. 11 – 12

13. An evil spirit from the Lord - I Samuel 16: 14

14. Played the harp - I Samuel 16: 23

15. 5 smooth stones and his sling - I Samuel 17: 40

16. Michal - I Samuel 18: 27

17. In a cave - I Samuel 24: 1 – 4

18. Abigail - I Samuel 25: 2 – 3, 39

19. Samuel - I Samuel 28: 11

20. The Philistines killed Saul's sons and the archers hit Saul badly wounding him. Saul took his sword and fell on it. - I Samuel 31: 1 – 4

10

Second Samuel

Answers on page 48

1. The Amalekite who came to David to tell him of the death of Saul and Jonathan brought what items that he had taken from Saul?

2. Who told Saul's daughter that he would transfer the kingdom from the house of Saul and establish the throne of David over Israel and over Judah?

3. Before making a covenant with Abner, what did David request Abner to bring to him?

4. When news came of the death of Saul and Jonathan, what happened to Mephibosheth, Jonathan's five year old son?

5. Who told David he acted foolishly and shamed himself by dancing in the streets as the Ark of God came into the city of David?

6. What was the name of the husband of Bathsheba?

7. When David learned Bathsheba was pregnant with his child what did he do?

8. After Bathsheba mourned over the death of her husband what happened to her?

9. Who did the Lord send to rebuke David over his actions with Bathsheba and Uriah?

10. What cost did David pay due to his actions with Bathsheba and Uriah?

11. What was the name of the second child born to David and Bathsheba?

12. Why did Absalom, son of David, have Amnon another son of David killed?

Answers – Chapter 10 – Second Samuel

1. Crown and a bracelet – II Samuel 1: 1 – 10

2. Abner - II Samuel 3: 1 – 10

3. To bring Michal, Saul's daughter, to him - II Samuel 3: 12 – 13

4. His nurse took him and fled and in her hurry dropped him causing him to become lame. - II Samuel 4: 4

5. Michal, Saul's daughter - II Samuel 6: 12 – 23

6. Uriah the Hittite - II Samuel 11: 3

7. He sent for Uriah from battle and told him to go home to be with his wife. When Uriah refused because the Ark of the Covenant and the servants of the Lord were camping in an open field and he didn't feel it was right for him to go to his home, David then sent him to the front line of the fiercest battle so he would die. - II Samuel 11: 1 – 15

8. She became the wife of David. - II Samuel 11: 26 – 27

9. Nathan - II Samuel 12: 1 – 10

10. The child of David and Bathsheba died. - II Samuel 12: 14, 18

11. Solomon - II Samuel 12: 24

12. For violating Absalom's sister Tamar - II Samuel 13: 32

11

First Kings

Answers on page 52 - 53

1. When David was advanced in years, who did King David vow would be king and sit on his throne in his place?

2. Who did Solomon form a marriage alliance with?

3. When God appeared to Solomon in a dream, what did God say to him?

4. What did Solomon ask God to give him?

5. When the two women came before Solomon both declaring a child was theirs, how did Solomon determine who the real mother was?

6. What gift was given to Solomon by the Lord?

7. What did Solomon build for the Lord which would keep the Ark of the Covenant?

8. The inner sanctuary of the house of the Lord was overlaid with what?

9. Who was the queen who hearing of the fame of Solomon came to test his knowledge?

10. In his old age, who turned Solomon's heart away from the Lord?

11. Who did the prophet Ahijah take from him his new cloak tearing it into 12 pieces telling him to take 10 pieces as the Lord God said He would tear the kingdom out of the hands of Solomon and give him 10 tribes?

12. When the people approached King Rehoboam and asked him to lighten the hard service his father Solomon had put on them, whose advice did Rehoboam take when answering the people: the elders who advised him to lighten the load or the young men he grew up with who advised him to add to the yoke?

13. What did Ahab do that was evil in the sight of the Lord, more than all who were before him?

14. When Elijah approached the widow from Zarephath during the drought, what did he ask of her?

15. When Elijah approached the widow for bread to eat, what did she tell him of her plans for herself and her son?

16. What did Elijah tell the widow the Lord would provide for her until rain returned to the earth?

17. What did Elijah do when the widow's son died?

18. How did Elijah show the sons of Israel whether the Lord was God or if it was Baal?

19. What did Naboth have that Ahab coveted?

20. Jezebel had Naboth stoned to death so Ahab could possess his vineyards. Because of this what did the Lord say would be her fate?

Answers – Chapter 11 – First Kings

1. Solomon – I Kings 1: 29 – 30

2. The Pharaoh, King of Egypt - I Kings 3: 1

3. "Ask what you wish Me to give you." - I Kings 3: 5

4. An understanding heart to judge people between good and evil - I Kings 3: 6 – 9

5. He asked for a sword to cut the child in two and to split the child between the two women. The true mother rather than having her child killed told Solomon to spare his life and give the child to the other woman. Then Solomon knew she was the child's mother. - I Kings 3: 16 – 27

6. Wisdom - I Kings 4: 29 – 34

7. Temple or house for the Lord - I Kings 6: 1, 19

8. Gold - I Kings 6: 21 – 22

9. Queen of Sheba - I Kings 10: 1

10. His wives - I Kings 11: 1 – 4

11. Jeroboam - I Kings 11: 28 – 31

12. The young men - I Kings 12: 3 – 15

13. He served and worshipped Baal and erected an altar for Baal and made the Asherah. - I Kings 16: 30 – 33

14. A drink of water and a piece of bread. - I Kings 17: 10

15. She was going to prepare the handful of flour that she and her son could eat and then die. - I Kings 17: 10 – 12

16. The bowl of flour shall not be exhausted, nor shall the jar of oil be empty. - I Kings 17: 13 – 16

17. He stretched himself upon the child three times and then called to the Lord and asked Him to return the child's life to him. - I Kings 17: 17 – 24

18. The followers of Baal cut up an ox and placed it on wood as did Elijah. They each called on their God and the one that answered with fire was the true God. - I Kings 18: 20 – 39

19. A vineyard – I Kings 21: 1 – 3

20. The dogs would eat her. - I Kings 21: 23

12

Second Kings

Answers on page 57 - 58

1. What act did Elijah do to divide the waters of Jordan?

2. As Elijah was about to be taken to heaven, what was Elisha's request of Elijah?

3. How was Elijah taken up to heaven?

4. How did the young lads mock Elisha?

5. When the widow cried to Elisha that her husband was dead and the creditor had come to take her two children as slaves and left her with only a jar of oil, what did Elisha tell her to do?

6. A prominent Shunammite offered Elisha food whenever he passed by and had her husband make an area for him to rest when he needed. What did Elisha give her in return for her kindness?

7. When the Shunammite woman's son died, what did Elisha do to

restore his life to him?

8. What sickness was Naaman, captain of the army of the King of Aram, inflected with?

9. What instructions did Elisha give to Naaman in order to cure him of his leprosy?

10. How did Jezebel die and then what happened to her body?

11. What was the fate of the 70 sons of Ahab?

12. When Athaliah the mother of Ahaziah saw that her son the king was dead, what heinous act did she commit?

13. Who saved Joash, the sole surviving offspring of Ahaziah?

14. How old was Jehoash when he became king?

15. As a man was being buried his body was cast into the grave of Elisha. When the man's body touched the bones of Elisha, what happened?

16. When Amaziah became king he killed his servants who had slain his father, but he did not kill the sons of the slayers. Why?

17. Why did God allow Israel to be taken into exile?

18. The Lord was angry with the sons of Israel and removed them from His sight. Only one tribe was left, which tribe was this?

19. What celebration did King Josiah reinstate?

20. Who killed King Josiah?

Answers – Chapter 12 – Second Kings

1. He took his mantle and folded it together and struck the waters. - II Kings 2: 7

2. To let a double portion of Elijah's spirit be upon him. - II Kings 2: 9

3. He was taken up by a whirlwind to heaven. - II Kings 2: 11

4. They called him, "You baldhead." - II Kings 2: 23

5. He told her to borrow vessels from neighbors and pour into the vessels her oil and the oil only stopped when there were no more vessels. He then told her to sell her oil and to pay the debt. - II Kings 4: 1 – 7

6. A son - II Kings 4: 8 – 17

7. He laid on the child, put his mouth on the mouth of the child, his eyes on the son's eyes, and his hands on the son's hands, and stretched himself on him. - II Kings 4: 18 – 37

8. Leprosy - II Kings 5: 1

9. Wash in the Jordan 7 times - II Kings 5: 10

10. Jehu told the officials who were on his side to throw her down from the window she was looking out. She was thrown from the window and the dogs ate her. - II Kings 9: 30 – 37

11. They were slaughtered and their heads were put in baskets and sent to Jezreel. Their heads were put at the entrance to the city of Jezreel. - II Kings 10: 1 – 11

12. She had all the royal offspring put to death so she would be Queen of Judah. - II Kings 11: 1

13. Ahaziah's sister, Jehosheba - II Kings 11: 1 – 3

14. 7 years of age - II Kings 11: 21

15. He revived - II Kings 13: 20 – 21

16. He followed what is written in the book of the Law of Moses as the Lord commanded which said, "The fathers shall not be put to death for the sons, nor the sons be put to death for the fathers; but each shall be put to death for his own sin." - II Kings 14: 1 – 6

17. The sons of Israel had sinned against the Lord their God. - II Kings 17: 6 – 18

18. The tribe of Judah - II Kings 17: 18

19. Passover - II Kings 23: 21 – 23

20. Pharaoh Neco - II Kings 23: 29

13

First Chronicles

Answers on page 62 - 63

1. Who were the sons of Abraham?

2. Who were the sons of Isaac?

3. Who were the twelve sons of Israel?

4. Who was the firstborn of Israel?

5. Who were the sons of Levi?

6. Who was the father of Aaron, Miriam, and Moses?

7. How was Israel enrolled, which is written in the Book of the Kings of Israel?

8. What tribe were the four chief gatekeepers, an office of trust, and over

the chambers of treasuries in the house of God?

9. Who defeated and killed the sons of Saul and also wounded Saul?

10. When the body of Saul was found, what was done with him?

11. When the Ark of God was returned to Israel, when they came to the threshing floor of Chidon the oxen nearly upset the Ark of God. Who put his hand out to hold the Ark angering the Lord?

12. Who stood against Israel causing David to take a census, a counting of the people?

13. In retribution for taking the census, what three choices did Gad, speaking for the Lord give David?

14. What was David's reply to the three choices given him?

15. What task was passed to Solomon before the death of David?

16. The sons of Moses were named among what tribe?

17. *Fill in the blank.* The Lord sad He would multiply Israel as the ____________ of heaven.

18. Who said this to his son, "Know the God of your father, and serve Him with a whole heart and a willing mind; for the Lord searches all

hearts, and understands every intent of the thoughts. If you seek Him, He will let you find Him; but if you forsake Him, He will reject you forever"?

Answers – Chapter 13 – First Chronicles

1. Isaac and Ishmael – I Chronicles 1: 28

2. Esau and Israel - I Chronicles 1: 34

3. Reuben, Simeon, Levi, Judah, Issachar, Zebulon, Dan, Joseph, Benjamin, Naphtali, Gad, and Asher - I Chronicles 2: 1

4. Reuben - I Chronicles 5: 1

5. Gershon, Kohath, and Merari - I Chronicles 6: 1

6. Amran - I Chronicles 6: 3

7. Genealogies - I Chronicles 9: 1

8. Levi, the Levites - I Chronicles 9: 26

9. Philistines - I Chronicles 10: 2 – 4

10. The Philistines stripped him and took his armor and head and placed them in the house of their gods. - I Chronicles 10: 8 – 10

11. Uzza - I Chronicles 13: 7 – 10

12. Satan - I Chronicles 21: 1

13. The three choices were:

1) 3 years of famine

2) 3 months to be swept away before your foes while the sword of your enemies overtakes you

3) 3 days of the sword of the Lord, pestilence in the land, and the angel of the Lord destroying throughout all the territory of Israel

- I Chronicles 21: 9 – 12

14. "Let me fall into the hand of the Lord, for His mercies are very great. But do not let me fall into the hand of man." He chose choice #3. - I

Chronicles 21: 13

15. To build a house for the Lord God of Israel - I Chronicles 22: 2 – 12

16. Levi - I Chronicles 23: 13 – 14

17. Stars - I Chronicles 27: 23

18. David said this to his son Solomon - I Chronicles 28: 9

14

Second Chronicles

Answers on page 66 - 67

1. What did Solomon pray for God to give him?

2. Where did Solomon build the house of the Lord?

3. Before the Ark of the Covenant was brought into the temple that Solomon built, where was the Ark kept?

4. Where in the temple was the Ark of the Covenant kept?

5. What was in the Ark of the Covenant?

6. When the Ark of the Covenant was brought into the temple the priests and the Levitical singers praised God, what then happened?

7. Why did the Queen of Sheba come to Jerusalem?

8. What were some of the gifts the Queen of Sheba gave to Solomon?

9. How far did Solomon's rule reach?

10. *Fill in the blank.* Hanani the seer said to Asa the King of Judah:"The eyes of the Lord move to and fro throughout the earth that He may strongly support those whose ___________ is completely His."

11. Ahab the king of Israel fought against Ramoth-gilead even though Micaiah, a prophet of God, advised him otherwise. Ahab in battle disguised himself so he would not be pursued. What happened to him during the battle?

12. Which king was responsible for cleansing the temple and had the people consecrate themselves, thus establishing the house of the Lord?

13. When Manasseh did evil in the sight of the Lord ignoring the Lord when He spoke to him and his people, the Lord brought the commanders of Assyria against him. What happened to Manasseh?

14. What did Hilkiah the priest discover when the temple was being repaired?

15. King Josiah after the book of the law of the Lord was found did what to ensure the people would know the words of the law?

Answers – Chapter 14 – Second Chronicles

1. He prayed for wisdom and knowledge. - II Chronicles 1: 8 – 10

2. Jerusalem on Mount Moriah - II Chronicles 3: 1

3. The city of David which is in Zion. - II Chronicles 5: 2

4. The priests brought the Ark into the inner sanctuary of the house, to the Holy of Holies, under the wings of the cherubim. - II Chronicles 5: 7

5. The two tablets (which Moses put there at Horeb, where the Lord made a covenant with the sons of Israel when they came out of Egypt. - II Chronicles 5: 10

6. The house of the Lord was filled with a cloud, the glory of the Lord filled the house of God. - II Chronicles 5: 11 – 14

7. To test Solomon with difficult questions. - II Chronicles 9: 1

8. 120 talents of gold, a great amount of spices, and precious stones - II Chronicles 9: 9

9. He was ruler over all the kings from the Euphrates River to the land of the Philistines and as far as the border of Egypt. - II Chronicles 9: 26

10. Heart - II Chronicles 16: 9

11. A man drew his bow at random and struck the king of Israel in a joint of his armor. He died. - II Chronicles 18: 28 – 34

12. King Hezekiah - II Chronicles 29: 5 – 6, 15, 35

13. He was bound with chains and taken to Babylon. He humbled himself and entreated God who listened and returned him to Jerusalem. - II Chronicles 33: 2 – 8, 10 – 13

14. The book of the law of the Lord given by Moses - II Chronicles 34: 14

15. He gathered all the elders of Judah and Jerusalem, went to the house of the Lord, and all the men of Judah, inhabitants of Jerusalem, priests, Levites, and all the people from the greatest to the least and read in their

hearing all the words of the book of the covenant found in the house of the Lord. - II Chronicles 34: 14 – 21, 29 – 30

15

Ezra

Answers on page 70

1. In the first year of Cyrus King of Perisa in order to fulfill the word of the Lord by the mouth of Jeremiah, what word did he send out in a proclamation?

2. Who worked on restoring the temple?

3. Work had been stopped on the temple, what made them resume their work?

4. Who did the adversaries who didn't want to see the temple built write to in order to have the work stopped?

5. Who destroyed the original temple Solomon built?

6. In Cyrus' decree in regards to rebuilding the temple, what did the decree say as far as how the rebuilding the temple was to be paid for?

7. *Fill in the blank.* Darius also issued a decree in regards to the rebuilding

of the temple. In his decree it stated that, 'Any man who violates this edict, a ___________ shall be drawn from his house and he shall be impaled on it and his house shall be made a refuse heap on account of this.'

8. What holiday did the exiles observe after the completion of the building of the temple?

9. King Artaxerxes issued a decree which stated that Ezra the priest, the scribe of the law of the God of heaven, according to his wisdom should appoint magistrates and judges. What was the role of the magistrates and judges?

10. What did Ezra proclaim before the people how they had been unfaithful?

Answers – Chapter 15 – Ezra

1. The Lord God gave him all the kingdom of the earth and appointed him to build the Lord God a house in Jerusalem. - Ezra 1: 1 – 2

2. Zerubbabel the son of Shealtiel, and Joshua the son of Jozadak, and the rest of their brothers, the priests, and the Levites, and all who came from the captivity to Jerusalem. - Ezra 3: 8

3. Prophets (Haggai and Zechariah) prophesied to the Jews. - Ezra 5: 1

4. Darius the king – Ezra 5: 3 – 17

5. Nebuchadnezzar, king of Babylon – Ezra 5: 12

6. From the royal treasury – Ezra 6: 4

7. Timber – Ezra 6: 11

8. Passover – Ezra 6: 19

9. To judge the people – Ezra 7: 25

10. They married foreign wives. - Ezra 10: 10

16

Nehemiah

Answers on page 73

1. What was Nehemiah's role to the king?

2. When King Artaxerxes asked Nehemiah why he was sad what was his answer?

3. When the king asked Nehemiah, "What would you request?," what was Nehemiah's desire?

4. Sanballat was angry when he learned the Jews were rebuilding the wall. What did he and Tobiah, the Arabs and Ammonites, and the Ashdodites conspire to do?

5. Those rebuilding the wall took their load with one hand and what did they hold in the other hand?

6. The wall was very large and the workers were separated on the wall from one another. What signal did they receive if they were needed to fight their enemies?

7. Who was appointed as governor in the land of Judah?

8. In the book of Moses, why was it written that no Ammonite or Moabite should ever enter the assembly of God?

Answers – Chapter 16 – Nehemiah

1. Cupbearer – Nehemiah 1: 11

2. The city, the place of my father's tombs lies desolate and the gates have been consumed with fire. - Nehemiah 2: 3

3. To go to Judah to rebuild it. - Nehemiah 4: 5

4. To fight against Jerusalem - Nehemiah 4: 1, 7 – 8

5. A weapon - Nehemiah 4: 16 – 18

6. The sound of the trumpet - Nehemiah 4: 19 – 20

7. Nehemiah - Nehemiah 5: 14

8. They did not meet the sons of Israel with bread and water, but hired Balsam to curse them. - Nehemiah 13: 1 – 2

17

Esther

Answers on page 76

1. When King Ahasuerus gave a banquet for his princes, nobles, and officers; what did Queen Vashti do that angered the king?

2. Why did Memucan a prince of Perisa and Media say that Queen Vashti's act of defiance would affect the action of the other women?

3. What was Queen Vashti's fate due to her act of defiance?

4. Who raised Esther as his own daughter?

5. Who did the king choose from all the virgins to replace Queen Vashti?

6. According to Mordecai's direction Esther did not make known her people or kindred. Who were her kindred?

7. How did Queen Esther save the life of the king, with the aid of Mordecai?

8. Who plotted against the Jews?

9. What was to be done to the Jews?

10. What did Mordecai request of Esther when he learned of the edict to destroy the Jews?

11. What happened to any man or woman who came to the king to the inner court who had not been summoned?

12. Mordecai told Esther, "Who knows whether you have not attained royalty for such a time as this." What did Esther request of the Jews before she approached the king?

13. What was Haman's fate?

14. What holiday was instituted for the Jews to celebrate the saving of the Jews from Haman?

Answers – Chapter 17 – Esther

1. She refused to come at the king's command. - Esther 1: 10 – 12

2. He said it would cause the other women to look with contempt on their husbands and they would act in the same manner towards their husbands. - Esther 1: 13 – 18

3. She was replaced and a new queen would take her place chosen from beautiful young virgins. - Esther 2: 1 – 4

4. Her uncle Mordeaci - Esther 2: 5 – 7

5. Esther - Esther 2: 17

6. Jews - Esther 2: 20

7. Mordecai learned of a plot that two of the king's officials planned to lay hands on the king. Mordecai told Queen Esther who informed the king in Mordecai's name. - Esther 2: 21 – 23

8. Haman - Esther 3: 1 – 6

9. They were to be destroyed, killed, and annihilate all the Jews and their possessions seized as plunder. - Esther 3: 13

10. He ordered her to go in to the king and plead for her people. - Esther 4: 8

11. They were put to death unless the king held out the golden scepter so they may live. - Esther 4: 11

12. Fast for 3 days and nights. - Esther 4: 13 – 16

13. He was hung on the gallows he had built to hang Mordecai from. - Esther 7: 2 – 10

14. Purim - Esther 9: 20 – 22

Poetry / Writings

18

Job

Answers on page 80

1. In the beginning of the book of Job, how was Job described?

2. When God asked Satan, "From where do you come?," how did Satan answer?

3. When Job was informed he had lost much, including his children; how did he respond?

4. Covered with boils, when Job's wife approached him and told him to curse God and die, what was Job's response?

5. Were Job's friends a comfort to him in his time of grief?

6. What type of man does Job say may not come before God's presence?

7. Why did Job's friends grow angry with him?

8. From where did God speak to Job?

9. Why was God displeased with Job's friends?

10. What was Job's fate after he prayed for his friends?

Answers – Chapter 18 – Job

1. Blameless, upright, fearing God and turning away from evil – Job 1: 1

2. From roaming the earth – Job 1: 6 – 7

3. He did not sin or blame God. He said, "Naked I came from my mother's womb, and naked I shall return there. The Lord gave and the Lord has taken away. Blessed be the name of the Lord." - Job 1: 13 – 22

4. "Shall we indeed accept good from God and not accept adversity?" - Job 2: 9 – 10

5. No – Job 6: 14 – 15, 19: 1 – 6, 19: 13 – 14

6. A godless man – Job 13: 16

7. Because Job was righteous in his own eyes and he justified himself before God – Job 32: 1 – 2

8. Out of the whirlwind – Job 38: 1

9. Because they did not speak of God what is right as Job did – Job 42: 7

10. God restored Job's fortunes. - Job 42: 10

19

Psalms

Answers on page 83

1. *Fill in the blank.* I will give ___________ to the Lord with all my heart.

2. In Psalm 15, a Psalm of David, name one of the traits that are mentioned for someone whose faith will never be shaken.

3. *Fill in the blanks.* Psalm 23: The Lord is my ___________, I shall not want. He makes me lie down in ___________ ___________; He leads me beside ___________ waters. He restores my ___________; He guides me in the path of ___________, For His names sake.

4. *Fill in the blank.* Psalm 25: To You, O Lord, I lift up my soul. O my God, in You I trust, Do not let me be ___________.

5. *Fill in the blanks.* Psalm 32: How blessed is he whose ___________ is forgiven, Whose ___________ is covered.

6. *Fill in the blanks.* Psalm 33: By the ___________ of the Lord the heavens were made, And by the ___________ of His mouth all their host.

7. *Fill in the blanks.* Psalm 37: Do not fret because of ____________, Be not envious toward wrongdoers. For they will wither quickly like the grass and fade like the green herb. Trust in the Lord and do ____________.

8. *Fill in the blank.* Psalm 37: The Lord knows the days of the blameless; And their inheritance will be ____________.

9. *Fill in the blank.* Psalm 37: Depart from evil, and do ____________.

10. *Fill in the blank.* Psalm 39: I will guard my ways, That I may not sin with my ____________; I will guard my mouth as with a muzzle.

11. *Fill in the blank.* Psalm 46: God is our refuge and strength, A very present help in ____________.

12. *Fill in the blanks.* Psalm 103: Bless the Lord, O my soul, And all that is within me, Bless His ____________ ____________.

13. *Fill in the blank.* Psalm 103: He has not dealt with us according to our sins, Nor rewarded us according to our iniquities. For as high as the heavens are above the earth, So great is His ____________ toward those who fear Him.

14. *Fill in the blank.* Psalm 117: It is better to take refuge in the Lord, than to trust in ____________.

15. *Fill in the blank.* Psalm 127: ____________ are a gift of the Lord; The fruit of the womb is a reward.

Answers – Chapter 19 – Psalms

1. Thanks – Psalm 9: 1

2. He who walks with integrity and works righteousness, speaks the truth, doesn't slander, does no evil to his neighbor or reproach against a friend, a sinner is despised, but one who honors those who fear the Lord, charges no interest, doesn't take a bribe; he is one whose faith will never be shaken. - Psalm 15: 1 – 5

3. Shepherd, green pastures, quiet, soul, righteousness - Psalm 23: 1 – 3

4. Ashamed - Psalm 25: 1 – 2

5. Transgression, sin - Psalm 32: 1

6. Word, breath - Psalm 33: 6

7. Evildoers, good - Psalm 37: 1 – 3

8. Forever - Psalm 37: 18

9. Good - Psalm 37: 27

10. Tongue - Psalm 39: 1

11. Trouble - Psalm 46: 1

12. Holy name - Psalm 103: 1

13. Lovingkindness - Psalm 103: 10 – 11

14. Man - Psalm 117: 8

15. Children - Psalm 127: 3

20

Proverbs

Answers on page 87 - 88

1. *Fill in the blank.* The fear of the Lord is the beginning of ___________.

2. *Fill in the blank.* If sinners entice you, do not ___________.

3. *Fill in the blank.* Do not forget my teaching, but let your heart keep My ___________.

4. *Fill in the blank.* Trust in the Lord with all your heart, and do not lean on your own ___________.

5. There are six things that the Lord hates, seven which are an abomination to Him. Name one of them.

6. *Fill in the blank.* Ill-gotten gains do not ___________.

7. *Fill in the blanks.* ___________ stirs up strife, but ___________ covers all transgressions.

8. *Fill in the blank.* A ____________ woman attains honor.

9. *Fill in the blank.* The ____________ of a man's hands will return to him.

10. *Fill in the blank.* The man who guards his mouth preserves his life; The one who opens wide his lips comes to ____________.

11. *Fill in the blank.* He who is slow to ____________ has great understanding.

12. *Fill in the blanks.* The eyes of the Lord are in every place, watching the ____________ and the ____________.

13. *Fill in the blank.* Before honor comes ____________.

14. *Fill in the blank.* A perverse man spreads ____________, and a slanderer separates intimate friends.

15. *Fill in the blank.* A joyful heart is good ____________.

16. *Fill in the blanks.* A fool's ____________ is his ruin, and his lips are the snare of his ____________.

17. *Fill in the blank.* A false witness will not go unpunished, and he who tells ____________ will not escape.

18. *Fill in the blank.* What is desirable in a man is his ___________.

19. What is the bond of a rich man and a poor man?

20. *Fill in the blank.* He who conceals his ___________ will not prosper, But he who confesses and forsakes them will find compassion.

Answers – Chapter 20 – Proverbs

1. Knowledge – Proverbs 1: 7

2. Consent – Proverbs 1: 10

3. Commandments – Proverbs 3: 1

4. Understanding – Proverbs 3: 5

5. Haughty eyes, a lying tongue, hands that shed innocent blood, a heart that devises wicked plans, feet that run rapidly to evil, a false witness who utters lies, and one who spreads strife among brothers. – Proverbs 6: 16 – 19

6. Profit – Proverbs 10: 2

7. Hate, love – Proverbs 10: 12

8. Gracious – Proverbs 11: 16

9. Deeds – Proverbs 12: 14

10. Ruin – Proverbs 13: 3

11. Anger – Proverbs 14: 29

12. Evil, good – Proverbs 15: 3

13. Humility – Proverbs 15: 33

14. Strife – Proverbs 16: 28

15. Medicine – Proverbs 17: 22

16. Mouth, soul – Proverbs 18: 7

17. Lies – Proverbs 19: 5

18. Kindness – Proverbs 19: 22

19. The Lord is the maker of them all. – Proverbs 22: 2

20. Transgressions – Proverbs 28: 13

21

Ecclesiastes

Answers on page 91

1. *Fill in the blank.* There is nothing ____________ under the sun.

2. The author of Ecclesiastes, inferred to be Solomon, set his mind to seek wisdom. When speaking of all the works under the sun, what were his thoughts on this subject?

3. 'The wise man's eyes are in his head, but the fool walks in darkness,' yet they both face the same fate, which is what?

4. *Fill in the blanks.* There is an appointed time for everything.

A time to give birth and a time to ____________.

A time to be ____________ and a time to speak.

A time to love and a time to ____________.

A time for war and a time for ____________.

5. Both man and beast will return to what?

6. What is said about man's lot, that he should be what?

7. What is better than an old, foolish king who no longer knows how to receive instruction?

8. What instructions are given in reference to bringing up a matter in the presence of God?

9. *Fill in the blank.* God has made both – the day of prosperity and the day of ___________.

10. There is not a righteous man on earth who has never done what?

Answers – Chapter 21 – Ecclesiastes

1. New – Ecclesiastes 1: 9

2. All is vanity and striving after wind. – Ecclesiastes 1: 12 – 15

3. They both die. – Ecclesiastes 2: 12 – 16

4. Die, silent, hate, peace – Ecclesiastes 3: 1 – 8

5. Dust – Ecclesiastes 3: 19 – 20

6. Happy – Ecclesiastes 3: 22

7. A poor yet wise lad - – Ecclesiastes 4: 13

8. (Guard your steps, draw near to listen.) Do not be hasty in word or impulsive in thought to bring up a matter in the presence of God. Let your words be few. – Ecclesiastes 5: 1 – 2

9. Adversity – Ecclesiastes 7: 14

10. Sinned - – Ecclesiastes 7: 20

22

Song of Solomon

Answers on page 93

1. What is the subject of the book '*Song of Solomon*' about?

2. What does Solomon compare the Shulammite bride to?

Answers – Chapter 22 – Song of Solomon

1. The love and marriage of Solomon and his Shulammite bride – Song of Solomon

2. His mare among the chariots of Pharaoh - – Song of Solomon 1: 9

Major Prophets

23

Isaiah

Answers on page 97

1. *Fill in the blanks.* Woe to those who call evil good, and good evil; Who substitute ___________ for light and light for ___________.

2. In Isaiah's vision what did the seraphim touch to Isaiah's lips to take away his iniquity and to have his sin forgiven?

3. In Isaiah's vision, what was Isaiah's commission from the Lord?

4. What did the Lord tell Ahaz that the sign He sent would be?

5. What did the Lord tell Ahaz the virgin would call the child's name?

6. Name one of the names the child would be called.

7. What sign did the Lord give to Isaiah to show He had heard Hezekiah's prayer and would add 15 years to his life?

8. The grass withers and the flower fades, but what stands forever?

9. *Fill in the blank.* We are the clay, and You are our ___________; And all of us are the work of Your hand.

10. *Fill in the blank.* Heaven is My throne and the earth is My ___________.

Answers – Chapter 23 – Isaiah

1. Darkness, darkness – Isaiah 5: 20

2. Burning coal – Isaiah 6: 5 – 7

3. In his vision the Lord told Isaiah to go and tell the people: "*Keep on listening, but do not perceive; Keep on looking, but do not understand.' "Render the hearts of this people insensitive, Their ears dull, And their eyes dim, Otherwise they might see with their eyes, Hear with their ears, Understand with their hearts, And return and be healed.*"

3. A virgin will be with child and bear a son. – Isaiah 7: 10 – 14

5. Immanuel – Isaiah 7: 14

6. Wonderful Counselor, Mighty God, Eternal Father, Prince of Peace– Isaiah 9: 6

7. He would cause the shadow on the stairway, which has gone down with the sun on the stairway of Ahaz, to go back ten steps. – Isaiah 38: 1 – 8

8. The word of our God – Isaiah 40: 7 – 8

9. Potter – Isaiah 64: 8

10. Footstool – Isaiah 66: 1

24

Jeremiah

Answers on page 101 - 102

1. What was Jeremiah's reaction when the word of the Lord told him he had been appointed as a prophet to the nations?

2. Why was Jeremiah sent to rebuke the families of the house of Israel?

3. What did the Lord use to compare the acts of Israel?

4. What did the Lord say Jerusalem would be called?

5. What message did Jeremiah give at the temple gate according to the word that came to him from the Lord?

6. *Fill in the blanks.* Jeremiah 9: 8 – 9. "Their ____________ is a deadly arrow; It speaks ___________; With his mouth one ____________ peace to his neighbor, But inwardly he sets an ambush for him: Shall I not punish him for those things?" declares the Lord.

7. The Lord said, "Let not a wise man boast of his wisdom, and let not the

mighty man boast of his might, let not a rich man boast of his riches..." What did the Lord say man should boast about?

8. *Fill in the blank.* The Lord is the true God; He is the living God and the everlasting ____________.

9. What did the Lord say would happen to the gods that did not make the heavens and the earth?

10. *Fill in the blank.* In Jeremiah's prayer to the Lord in reference to the people of Israel, he said, "You are near to their lips, But far from their ____________.

11. For judgment, what four types of doom did the Lord appoint over the people of Judah?

12. *Fill in the blank.* Thus says the Lord, "Cursed is the man who trusts in ____________, And makes flesh his strength, And whose heart turns away from the Lord.

13. What did the Lord God of Israel compare the captives of Judah and Zedekiah king of Judah and his officials to?

14. Why did the prophets and the priests appeal to the officials and the people for a death sentence for Jeremiah?

15. What did Jeremiah proclaim to the people to do when they plotted to kill him?

16. Why was Jeremiah's life spared?

17. Which king imprisoned Jeremiah for prophesying?

18. The Lord God instructed Jeremiah to write on a scroll all the words he spoke to him about Judah and the nations. What did the king do when it was read to him?

19. What was God's retribution to the king for destroying the scroll?

20. Who saved Jeremiah from the cistern?

Answers – Chapter 24 – Jeremiah

1. That he didn't know how to speak, as he was just a youth. - Jeremiah 1: 6

2. For their apostasy - Jeremiah 2: 4 – 19

3. A harlot - Jeremiah 3: 1 – 2

4. 'The Throne of the Lord' - Jeremiah 3: 17

5. Amend your ways and your deeds - Jeremiah 7: 1 – 3

6. Tongue; deceit; speaks - Jeremiah 9: 8 – 9

7. That he understands and knows the Lord, (that He is the Lord who exercises lovingkindness, justice, and righteousness on earth; for the Lord delights in these things.) - Jeremiah 9: 23 – 24

8. King - Jeremiah 10: 10

9. They will perish from the earth and from under the heavens. - Jeremiah 10: 11

10. Mind - Jeremiah 12: 2

11. The sword to slay, the dogs to drag off, and the birds of the sky and the beasts of the earth to devour and destroy - Jeremiah 15: 3

12. Mankind - Jeremiah 17: 5

13. Two baskets of figs – good figs in comparison to the captives and bad figs compared to the King of Judah and his officials - Jeremiah 24: 1 – 10

14. He prophesied against the city. - Jeremiah 26: 7 – 11

15. For them to amend their ways and deeds and obey God (as it was the Lord God who sent him to prophesy). He told them to do with him as was good and right in their sight, but if they put him to death, they would have innocent blood on their hands. - Jeremiah 26: 12 – 15

16. The officials and people told the priests and prophets that he was speaking in the name of the Lord their God. - Jeremiah 26: 16

17. King Zedekiah, king of Judah - Jeremiah 32: 1 – 5

18. Cut it and throw it in the fire until it was consumed - Jeremiah 36: 1 – 3, 20 – 23

19. He would have no heirs to sit on the throne of David and his dead body would be cast out to the heat of the day and frost of the night. He, his descendants, and servants would be punished. - Jeremiah 36: 30 – 31

20. An Ethiopian eunuch, Ebed-melich - Jeremiah 38: 6 – 13

25

Lamentations

Answers on page 104

1. What does the author of Lamentations compare the lonely city of Zion to?

2. *Fill in the blank.* Better are those slain with the sword, Than those slain with ____________.

3. What does Jeremiah pray for?

Answers – Chapter 25 – Lamentations

1. A widow – Lamentations 1:1

2. Hunger – Lamentations 4: 9

3. Mercy – Lamentations 5: 1 – 22

26

Ezekiel

Answers on page 107

1. From Ezekiel's vision, describe the figures he saw that resembled living beings.

2. How did the living beings from Ezekiel's vision move?

3. What did God tell Ezekiel to eat?

4. What duty did God appoint to Ezekiel?

5. *Fill in the blank.* Ezekiel 7: 25. When anguish comes, they will seek ____________, but there will be none.

6. How many executioners were called upon to cleanse Israel?

7. When the executioners were sent out, who were they told not to touch?

8. After the executioners slayed all without the mark on their foreheads, who was left standing?

9. What were the four severe judgments against Jerusalem God spoke of?

10. *Fill in the blank.* Ezekiel 18:4. All souls are mine. The soul who sins will ____________.

11. If the wicked man turns from all his sins, observes the Lord God's statutes he shall live. What about his past transgressions?

12. What will happen to the righteous man who turns away from his righteousness and sins?

13. The Lord God wishes for all to repent and make a new heart and spirit and live, for each will be judged according to his deeds. What is God's will for us?

14. *Fill in the blank.* "According to your ways and according to your ____________ I will judge you," declares the Lord God.

15. What happened in the valley that was full of bones?

Answers – Chapter 26 – Ezekiel

1. They had human form. They each had four faces and four wings. Their feet were like calf's hoofs. They had the look of polished bronze. Under their wings they had human heads. Their faces didn't turn, but looked straight ahead. They had the face of a man, the face of a lion, the face of a bull, and the face of an eagle. - Ezekiel 1: 4 – 10

2. Wheels - Ezekiel 1: 15 – 21

3. A scroll written on it were lamentations, mourning, and woe. - Ezekiel 2: 8 – 10

4. Watchman to the house of Israel - Ezekiel 3: 17

5. Peace - Ezekiel 7: 25

6. 6 - Ezekiel 9: 1 – 2

7. Any man with a mark on his forehead - Ezekiel 9: 4 – 6

8. 1, Ezekiel - Ezekiel 9: 3 – 8

9. Sword, famine, wild beasts, and plague - Ezekiel 14: 21

10. Die - Ezekiel 18: 4

11. They will not be remembered. - Ezekiel 18: 21 – 22

12. All his righteous deeds will not be remembered. - Ezekiel 18: 24

13. To repent and live - Ezekiel 18: 30 – 32

14. Deeds - Ezekiel 24: 14

15. God told Ezekiel to prophesy over the bones and God put sinews on the bones, covered them with skin, and put the breath of life in them. - Ezekiel 37: 1 – 10

27

Daniel

Answers on page 110 - 111

1. When King Nebuchadnezzar ordered his chief of officials to choose from some of the sons of Israel, of the royal family, and of nobles to serve in the king's personal service, what were some of the requirements of these young men?

2. What names were Daniel, Hananiah, Mishael, and Azariah given by the commander of the officials?

3. The young men chosen to serve in the king's personal service were fed the king's choice food and wine. What was Daniel's request of food and drink for himself and Hananiah, Mishael, and Azariah?

4. When the king had a dream, he wished to have the dream interpreted. He called forth magicians, conjurers, sorcerers, and the Chaldeans to interpret his dream. In order to not be deceived by their interpretations, what was his request of them?

5. Who revealed to the king his dream and it's interpretations?

6. Why were Shadrach, Meshach, Abed-nego ordered to be cast into a furnace of blazing fire?

7. Daniel's three friends were bound and cast into the fire. What did the king see when he looked into the furnace?

8. In King Nebuchadnezzar's dream of a tree that was large and strong but then chopped down with it's stump and roots left in the ground, how was this dream interpreted by Daniel or Belteshazzar?

9. Who ruled after King Nebuchadnezzar?

10. The fingers of a man's hand appeared before Belshazzar and began writing on the wall of the king's palace. What was the interpretation of the handwriting on the wall?

11. What was the commission the commissioners and satraps presented to the king in order to try to rid themselves of Daniel?

12. When the men approached the king with news that Daniel defied his petition and continued praying to his god, what was the king's reaction?

13. When Daniel was cast into the lion's den the king fasted. In the morning he called to Daniel from outside the lion's den to see if Daniel's god had saved him. What response did the king receive?

Answers – Chapter 27 – Daniel

1. They were to have no defects, good-looking, show intelligence, endowed with understanding and discerning knowledge and had the ability to serve in the king's court. - Daniel 1: 3 – 4

2. Daniel became Belteshazzar, Hananiah became Shadrach, Mishael became Meshach, Azariah became Abed-nego - Daniel 1: 6 – 7

3. Vegetables and water - Daniel 1: 8 – 16

4. To tell him what he dreamed. - Daniel 2: 1 – 11

5. Daniel through God in heaven. - Daniel 2: 12 – 30

6. They refused to bow and worship the golden image the king had set up. - Daniel 3: 1 – 18

7. He saw four men untied and walking about in the midst of the fire. The appearance of the fourth was like a son of the gods. - Daniel 3: 24 – 25

8. The king was the tree who had grown great and strong, an angelic watcher said to chop down the tree leaving it's stump and roots, and said the king would share with the beasts of the field and be given grass to eat as cattle for seven periods of time until the king recognizes that the Most High is ruler over all and bestows it on whomever He wishes. The king's kingdom would be assured to him after he recognized it is Heaven that rules. - Daniel 4: 10 – 26

9. The king's son, Belshazzar - Daniel 5: 1 – 2

10. God has numbered your kingdom and put an end to it. You have been weighed on the scales and found deficient. Your kingdom has been divided and given over to the Medes and Persians. - Daniel 5: 5, 25 – 28; 5: 1 – 36

11. The king should establish a statute and enforce an injunction that anyone who makes a petition to any god or man other than the king should be cast into the lion's den for thirty days. - Daniel 6: 1 – 7

12. He was deeply distressed but unable to deliver Daniel due to the petition being unable to be changed. - Daniel 6: 10 – 15

13. Daniel told him God sent His angel and shut the lions' mouths. - Daniel 6: 19 – 23

Minor Prophets

28

Hosea

Answers on page 114

1. *Fill in the blank.* The number of the sons of Israel will be like the ____________ of the sea, Which cannot be measured or counted.

2. What were the forefathers of Israel referred to?

3. *Fill in the blank.* Whoever is wise, let him understand these things; Whoever is discerning, let him know them. For the ways of the Lord are right, and the righteous will walk in them, But transgressors will ____________ in them.

Answers – Chapter 28 – Hosea

1. Sand – Hosea 1: 10

2. The earliest fruit on the fig tree in it's first season. - – Hosea 9: 10

3. Stumble – Hosea 14: 9

29

Joel

Answers on page 116

1. *Fill in the blanks.* I will display wonders in the sky and on the earth, Blood, fire, and columns of smoke. The sun will be turned into ____________ and the moon into ____________, Before the great and awesome day of the Lord comes.

Answers – Chapter 29 – Joel

1. Darkness, blood – Joel 2: 30 – 31

30

Amos

Answers on page 118

1. *Fill in the blanks.* He who made the ___________ and ___________ and changes deep darkness into morning, Who also darkens day into night, Who calls for the waters of the sea, And pours them out on the surface of the earth, The Lord is His name.

2. *Fill in the blank.* "Behold, days are coming," declares the Lord God, "When I will send a famine on the land, Not a famine for bread or a thirst for water, But rather a famine for hearing the ___________ of the Lord.

Answers – Chapter 30 – Amos

1. Pleiades, Orion - Amos 5: 8

2. Words – Amos 8: 11

31

Obadiah

Answers on page 120

1. *Fill in the blanks.* For the day of the Lord draws near on all the nations. As you have done (it will be done) ___________ ___________. Your dealings will return on your own head.

Answers – Chapter 31 – Obadiah

1. To you. - Obadiah 1: 15

32

Jonah

Answers on page 122

1. The word of God came to Jonah telling him to go to what city?

2. Jonah disobeyed God and by ship headed to Tarshish. When the men aboard the ship feared the ship would break up due to the storm on the sea, what did Jonah tell the men to do in order to calm the sea?

3. What happened to Jonah once he was thrown into the sea?

4. How long was Jonah in the stomach of the fish?

5. After Jonah prayed to God from the stomach of the fish, what was the Lord's next action?

Answers – Chapter 32 – Jonah

1. Ninevah – Jonah 1: 1 – 2

2. Throw him into the sea – Jonah 1: 4 – 12

3. A great fish swallowed Jonah and he was in the stomach of the fish. - Jonah 1: 15 – 17

4. 3 days and 3 nights – Jonah 1: 17

5. He commanded the fish to vomit Jonah onto dry land. - Jonah 2: 10

33

Micah

Answers on page 124

1. In the book of Micah, what does it say the Lord requires of man?

2. Son treats father contemptuously, Daughter rises up against her mother, Daughter-in-law against her mother-in-law. Who does it say are a man's enemies?

3. *Fill in the blank.* A God who pardons inequity and passes over rebellious acts who doesn't retain His anger forever, because He delights in unchanging ___________.

Answers – Chapter 33 – Micah

1. To do justice, to love kindness, and to walk humbly with your God – Micah 6: 8

2. The men of his own household – Micah 7: 6

3. Love – Micah 7: 18

34

Nahum

Answers on page 126

1. Who does God take vengeance on?

2. *Fill in the blank.* The Lord will by no means leave the ___________ unpunished.

Answers – Chapter 34 – Nahum

1. His adversaries – Nahum 1: 2

2. Guilty – Nahum 1: 3

35

Habakkuk

Answers on page 128

1. *Fill in the blank.* As for the ___________ one, His soul is not right within him.

Answers – Chapter 35 – Habakkuk

1. Proud – Habakkuk 2: 4

36

Zephaniah

Answers on page 130

1. Zephaniah was the son of who?

2. What did the Lord declare He would remove from the face of the earth?

3. What did the Lord say He would do with man at the time of the judgment of Judah?

4. What were the people told they should do before the day the Lord's anger came upon them?

Answers – Chapter 36 – Zephaniah

1. Cush – Zephaniah 1: 1

2. "I will completely remove all things." – Zephaniah 1: 2

3. Cut off man from the face of the earth – Zephaniah 1: 3

4. Seek the Lord – Zephaniah 2: 2 – 3

37

Haggai

Answers on page 132

1. *Fill in the blanks.* The word of the Lord came to Haggai, the prophet and messenger of the Lord, and the Lord said, "You have sown ____________, but harvest ____________."

2. What did the Lord say to rebuild?

3. When Haggai, messenger of the Lord, gave Zerubbabel son of Shealtiel, and Joshua the son of Jehozadak, the high priest, and the people the Lord's message, how did they respond?

Answers – Chapter 37 – Haggai

1. Much, little - Haggai 1: 3 – 6

2. The temple - Haggai 1: 7 – 8

3. They obeyed the voice of the Lord and showed reverence for the Lord - Haggai 1: 12

38

Zechariah

Answers on page 134

1. What did the angel tell Zechariah the meaning was behind "a man riding a red horse standing amongst the myrtle trees in the ravine with a red sorrel and white horse behind him"?

2. *Fill in the blank.* Let none of you devise ____________ in your heart against another.

Answers – Chapter 38 – Zechariah

1. These are those the Lord sent to patrol the earth – Zechariah 1: 8 – 10

2. Evil - Zechariah 8: 17

39

Malachi

Answers on page 136

1. The oracle of the word of the Lord to Israel came through Malachi. The Lord said, “A son honors his father, and a servant his master. Then if I am a father, where is My honor?” - What was the sin of the priests the Lord rebuked them for?

2. In the Lord's rebuke to the priests they were told that the lips of a priest should preserve knowledge and what should men receive from them?

3. Instead of the priests instructing man, what message did the Lord give the priests that their ways were causing men to do?

4. After the Lord's rebuke, then those who feared the Lord spoke to one another, and the Lord gave attention and heard it. What was written with the names of those who feared and esteemed the Lord's name?

5. Those who were included in the book of remembrance, what did the Lord say would be their fate?

Answers – Chapter 39 – Malachi

1. Their offerings – Malachi 1: 6 – 14

2. Instruction – Malachi 2: 7

3. To stumble – Malachi 2: 8

4. Book of remembrance – Malachi 3: 16

5. "They will be mine," said the Lord. "I will spare them." - The Lord will distinguish between the righteous and the wicked, between one who serves God and one who does not serve Him. – Malachi 3: 17 – 18

Be sure to follow up with

"The Big Book of New Testament Trivia"

also by Cheryl Pryor

www.ingramcontent.com/pod-product-compliance
Lightning Source LLC
LaVergne TN
LVHW021345080426
835508LV00020B/2115
* 9 7 8 1 8 8 6 5 4 1 3 3 7 *